The Stamp Collection

Dennis Stamp

DEDICATION

My ever suffering wife Debbie. My good friend Terry Funk. My entire family. And the people of Scotland for making an old man feel important again.

CONTENTS

Acknowledgments   I

1   Japan   3

2   Pistol Pez Whatley   9

3   Fear   17

4   Tough Guy   23

5   Ego   29

6   Movie Star   33

7   Haystacks Calhoun   39

8   Bryant Gumbel   45

9   The Match   51

10   Terry & Breck   61

FROM THE DESK OF TERRY FUNK

Dennis Stamp is a great friend of mine, and a hell of a nice guy. He will do anything for anybody and it's great to see him finally get the recognition he deserves. His legend in Amarillo will never tire, but I am glad to see it is continuing worldwide for everyone to see, especially in Scotland, where he seems to have made a new home. Thank you to everyone who has made my good friend feel like more than just an old man, he is a wrestler again.

Terry Funk

I'M NOT BOOKED

I've been hooked and crooked and overlooked
I'm not fully cooked
I am under booked
I'm not booked
I'm not booked

Around the world I did look
to find the one who took
the belt I forsook,
but I'm not booked.

The belt was mine to hold,
the match had been ice cold.
A proud territory had been sold,
a championship had been stold
and I know I'm not too old,
but I'm not booked.

A main event is the place to be,
anywhere on the card is ok with me.
It's not that I'm the best you see,
it's just a match is what I need,
but I'm not booked.

In dressing rooms everywhere you will see,
all the things I won't be.
A stooge, a snitch or a referee,
I'd rather work for free.

BUT, I'M NOT BOOKED.....

1 JAPAN

In the sixties and seventies, the place to wrestle was Japan. They paid all travel and hotel costs. More importantly they paid well. The tours were only four to six weeks long. If you were good enough you could go back two or three times a year. The lowest pay for Americans was six hundred dollars a week. Stars got $1000.00 to $1500.00. Big stars could get as much as $2000.00 a week.

The year was 1971. The minimum wage in the US was $1.25 an hour. So, Japan paid big money and $600.00 a week was BIG money to me.

It was the last week of October 1971. I'd had my first match with Joe Turco in Thunder Bay, Ontario, Canada on August 9, 1971. To say I was green would have been a gross understatement. I was real green to the other guys. They were all ten to twenty year veterans. Two other Americans, Red Bastien and Bull Bullinski, Two men from Spain, who spoke no English and Mario who was from Italy by way of Argentina. He spoke English]sh and Spanish and he was an old friend of Red Bastein.

We sort of paired up out of the ring. The two Spaniards, Red and Mario, and me and Bull were the teams. This was fine with me. I liked all the guys, especially Bull.

Now it's a rite of passage for wrestlers to ride rookies hard. Boy those guys did. It started the first night. The only place open to eat was a sushi bar. I was twenty five years old and had no idea people ate raw fish. They got me good with the octopus. In Japanese it's pronounced "taco".

"Hey kid," Red said. "You like tacos don't you? Just order tacos."

Ugh! Raw octopus slices. They looked like rubber and tasted worse.

Another night, they got me drinking sake. The next morning after the sake I woke up face down on the floor of my hotel room. I was still dressed. I had on a suit coat even shoes and socks. Talk about a headache. My whole body had a headache! I've never gone near sake again.

On this tour we had matches every night. Red, Bull, or Mario would be on top. The Spaniards were usually a team. I was the lowest foreigner on the card. I mostly wrestled the up and coming Japanese wrestlers, who were referred to as the Young Boys. The young boys referred to me as "cembluto".

The fans in Japan were different. They were very quiet. Unlike American fans that screamed and yelled at the matches; the Japanese fans just watched. It made the matches harder. American wrestling almost depends on the fans. If no one cheers for you or boos at you, then something is wrong with the match. The lack of verbal reaction had an impact on the matches. The older guys just slowed everything down in the ring. Me, I sped up. I was inexperienced. I was well trained and I knew how to wrestle. I liked lots of action in the ring.

As the tour continued, I started moving up in the card. Television was big money for the promoters. They only showed one match. By the end of November, I was doing the television matches. The last week of the tour, I was in the main event. Red Bastein was my partner against Kobeoshi and Kusatsu, Japans two biggest stars. I loved that!

I thought the match went well. Near the end of the match, Red was in the ring with Kobeoshi when Kusatsu jumped in the ring.

"Get him out of the ring!" Red hollered at me. Reds' plan was one on one.

I jumped in the ring. Kusatsu grabbed me and hit me with some big chops. They had done that to me all night. They wanted to let the rookie know who was boss. That didn't bother me. In fact, I liked it. It was a chance to earn respect. It also opened the door for me to hit hard.

However, if there had been a hit count or a velocity measure, I would have lost both. I didn't care. I knew I could take it. I was happy just being in the main event. To get Kusatsu out of Reds' way, I went to the ropes. He threw me out to the floor. Then, he came out after me.

He had me up against the ring hitting me with big chops. I was practically numb to the chops. I was keeping him busy the hard way. I was sort of drooped over the ring with the Great Kusatsu standing over me.

A little man, maybe about 4' 10", stepped out from behind Kusatsu. The Japanese fans were always so polite and quiet; the sight of this little man didn't alarm me. He wasn't half the size of the big wrestler who was pounding on me.

In a split second I saw a brown paper sack in his hand. "Pop" he hits me in the face with it. He had a bottle of whiskey in the bag. The smell of whiskey was immediate. The blow from the bottle didn't hurt.

My first thought was, 'so that's what it feels like to get hit with a whiskey bottle'. What a waste of whiskey. When I put my hands on my face, my hands were covered with blood. I had a large gash on my forehead. The bridge of my nose was split open with cuts and broken glass all over my body. The blood was pouring out of my forehead. I cupped my hands and was catching my blood. "What are you doing?" I asked myself. "You can't put it back!"

By the time I got all the way around the ring, it hit me. "Where is that little SOB". By then the police were leading him away. The match was still going on. Red hadn't seen what happened.

"What happened to you kid?" he then pulled up the front of my hair and looked at my face. "Your eyes okay?" He told me "Get a towel or something to stop the bleeding."

Then it hit me – fear. I'm going to bleed to death. I was really scared. I saw a nurses table. There were two Japanese nurses in white uniforms and white hats. What luck I thought. I had never seen nurses on duty at any wrestling matches before: amateur or professional. I went to the little table where they were sitting. When they saw me coming, they took off running. Now I was really scared. Now one spoke English and no one would. I'm going to bleed to death a long way from home I thought.

Finally Bullinski found me. He had a towel. It helped but it wouldn't stop the bleeding. I was getting more scared. We got on the bus that had brought us to the matches. It seemed to take the other guys forever to get on the bus.

In the meantime, my drear friend Frank shields – AKA – Bull Bullinski, calmed me down. He knew how scared I was. He stayed with me. He tried to make me laugh. I finally came back to earth a little. He was truly a lifesaver.

We finally left. I thought we'd never get to the hospital. When we got there I wasn't impressed. The hospital liked like an old house. Two nurses met me at the door. These girls were about 19 or 20. They were my real saviors. They didn't speak English. I didn't speak Japanese. I've never communicated with anyone so well before or since. The nurses knew how scared I was. They put me right at ease without saying a word. They cleaned the wounds and picked the glass of f of me. I don't know exactly all that they did. It wasn't one particular thing. Whit just their hands I knew I was going to be okay.

My forehead was stitched. I had a metal clip holding the bridge of my nose together. The doctor then wrapped my head with gauze bandages and tape. I looked like a mummy. I was not supposed to get my head wet. I had blood, sweat, tears and whiskey in my hair. I smelled bad, but I was happy to be alive!

One of the ceremonies at the matches was flowers. Each man in the main event got a big bouquet of flowers. Red didn't want any flowers, so I took his and mine and put them on the bus before the match started. I had planned to hand them out back at the hotel. As the two little nurses walked me to the front door, I remembered the flowers. I had two large bouquets probably, two dozen roses in each one. I gave each nurse a bouquet. They were standing there still smiling as we drove away. I'll never forget those two girls.

The next day I had to go to the police station in downtown Tokyo. When I saw the little man in the jail cell, he looked even smaller. He was crying and he looked scared to death. I felt sorry for him. I have always thought it was my fault. How could I have let it happen? As a wrestler, I must take care of myself.

I did not press charges. Now my tour was over, with only two days left on the tour, they sent me home.

Before I left I assured them I wanted to come back to Japan. At that last meeting no one spoke much English except me.

I thought what they said behind those smiles was don't call us, we'll call you.

I guess what they meant was written on the whiskey bottle:

NO DEPOSIT

NO RETURN

I have never been back to Japan.

Dory Funk Jr.

Dory Funk Jr. He's the real thing.
The praises of him I will always sing.
There's nothing he couldn't do in the ring,
of professional wrestling he was the king.

He won't take a step back that I can say.
You better be ready, he's not there to play.
If you are not with it your body will pay.
My advice is do it his way.

If you open the door for him just a crack,
that weakness becomes his point of attack.
Of courage and strength he does not lack,
be careful or you'll end up flat on your back.

He's a great father, that's easy to see,
his first born son is named Dory Funk 3.
He's a medical doctor now isn't that neat,
the sick and the wounded he does treat.

The Dory Funk legend will not go away,
I worship the man still to this day.
For all that he taught me I'll never repay,
so a long life and good health for Dory, I pray.

2 PISTOL PEZ WHATLEY

Pistol Pez was one of my favorite wrestlers and a dear friend. Friendship is a real treasure. It can't be bound by time or distance. In life there are only moments in time. Since Professional Wrestling is larger than life, so are its moments.

Pez and I first met in the Mid-south Wrestling territory. It was a large territory which covered: Oklahoma, Arkansas, Mississippi, Louisiana and parts of Texas. They ran three tours a night.

One Saturday night Pez and I were booked in Greenwood, Mississippi. We both stayed in Bossier City, Louisiana which meant we had a 265 mile trip and back.

We were from different worlds. Pez (an African-American) was born in Kentucky and grew up in Alabama. I grew up in the all-white world of Northern Minnesota.

What drew us together was amateur wrestling. We had both wrestled and played football in college. That was rare in Professional Wrestling. Some people called us real wrestlers. Other people in the business called us shooters. We had only known each other for a few weeks so this trip was our first time spent together.

On the first part of the trip, we were alpha males. We each talked and bragged about our athletic exploits. It was fun and something we couldn't talk about in front of the other wrestlers.

It was the summer of 1972. Pez had grown up in the Deep South. He had been a college student in the sixties and knew all about segregation and racism first hand.

In school he'd been in a demonstration where fire hoses were turned on the students. His grandmother had been in a "Grandmother Sit-In." The police turned the dogs on them. Pez's grandmother was scratched by one of the dogs.

Pez was polite, personable, and bright and had a quick smile. Any bitterness he may have felt didn't show.

Greenwood was a small town. It had a large African American population. Most of our fans were African American.

That night the house was full. There were probably about a thousand people; most had come to see Pez. They were not disappointed. Pez had a high octane, high flying style. He was handsome, well built, athletic, a real super hero.

The fans stood screaming when he first came into view. They screamed through the whole match. They were still screaming when he got back into the dressing room.

The dressing room was small. It had hooks on the wall for your clothes and boards coming out of the walls for seating.

Pez was sitting next to me, he was pumped. He knew he'd had a hell of a match.

Just then Bobby Couthen, the promoter, burst into the dressing room. Bobby was the State Wrestling Commissioner, Chief of the local Fire Department, and he owned the building.

He ran into the dressing room that night very excited. You could almost see dollar signs in his eyes.

"Did you see that there (N) he gushed. That there (N)" now he was eye to eye with Pez "that there, that there colored boy!" he finally stammered.

I was sitting next to Pez. His body stiffened like a board. I put my hand on his thigh and pushed him back down on the bench.

"Easy does it" I said calmly. "Let's be calm" I continued trying to hold him down.

The promoter did an about face and was out the door. We didn't see him again that night.

We had a long ride home. Pez was real quiet. After about ten or fifteen miles he started talking.

"Colored Boy," "Colored Boy," "Colored Boy" he said again. "Didn't he just say the word?" he said to me, his head bent. "I'm not a Boy, I'm nobody's Boy" he stated as he straightened, "I'm nobody's Boy" he stated firmly.

We were out away from town so I pulled off the road. It was solid forests, trees everywhere.

"Okay, Pez" I said. "I want you to scream."

"What?" he asked.

"Scream" I said.

"Scream what?" he asked.

"I don't care. Boy, The Word, swear words, anything you want. As loud as you can."

He cocked his head, looked at me kind of funny and walked over to the trees.

He yelled. And then he yelled again. He probably scared the birds and the squirrels for miles.

We got back on the road and started talking again. "Do you know what you did tonight?" I asked. "You gave the people something they haven't seen before."

"Well," he said to me "I brought my knife."

"What?" I asked shocked.

"Do you want to see it?" he asked.

11

"No," I said. "No, no. Why did you bring a knife?"

"I was gonna cut him," Pez said.

"Cut him? I said "you didn't know he was going to say that."

"Not him" he said.

"Who?" I asked.

"Alex Perez" he came back.

"Why?" I asked.

"I was on a trip with Alex. The car got a flat tire and when the driver got out to fix it, Perez hollered at him 'don't get out. Let the Boy do it.'

Now I had to think fast. "You've never cut anyone, have you?" I said firmly.

"No, not yet" he replied.

"I didn't think so" I said. "Pez, look" I started. "I can't know how you feel, but I know that you're mad. Let's look at the whole situation."

First of all: NO KNIFE. Keep it in your room or hide it in your trunk. Don't keep it in your wrestling bag. Think of it Pez, a black man with a knife. This is the South. Any kind of trouble and you're gone. And please don't tell the other wrestlers.

Let's talk about your match. It was probably the best match anyone ever had in Greenwood. There were fans that waited a lifetime to see a super hero who looked like them. Pez, you gave older people satisfaction and you gave young people hope.

"Yeah, and what did I get?" he asked somberly.

"You got a lot of love from a lot of people" I said.

"Yeah, and a lot of hate from the promoter" he replied.

"Okay, I said. "Let's take the promoter. Is he a jerk? Even he thinks so tonight." "Bobby's a middle aged southern white man. He was born into racism. He's really not a bad guy." I said. "He just said the worst possible thing at the worst possible moment."

Pez mumbled something. "Dumb ole cracker" was the part I heard.

"Here's what's going to happen" I said. "The promoter will act like it never happened." I paused. "So will you, Pez."

As I said this his head turned toward me. He stared not saying a word.

"Here's the deal, my friend. We're the dancers and he owns the stage."

Now I said let's talk about Perez.

Alex Perez was about 5'8" and close to 300 pounds. He'd been a Golden Gloves boxer and he thought he was tough. He was lazy, out of shape, not liked and a cheap shot artist.

"Pez, you would never need a knife for Perez, you could kill him with your bare hands."

"What am I supposed to do?" he finally asked confused and disgusted.

Good, I thought, now he's serious.

"Okay, Pez, here's what you do. You're booked against Alex next week. Now don't say anything to him. During the match run him, work him hard, tire him out, it won't be hard to do. Right before the end of the match back him into the corner and tag him."

"Do what?" he looked surprised.

"Tag him" I said. "Hit him in the head. Don't kill him. Just leave a mark. It won't stay on his face that long, but it will stay in his head."

As he was getting out of the car that night he asked me if I was serious. "Will it work?" he asked.

"Sure it will" I said. "SNAP" echoed in the car as I popped my fist into my open hand. "I speak from experience."

I saw Pez about a week later. When he saw me his smile could have lit a football stadium. "I heard all about it" I told him. "You know the hotline is alive and well."

Finally, he said "I never thought one punch could make that much difference."

One punch or one word, I thought to myself.

"Pez, keep that good feeling." I said. "Always keep the good."

Pez went on to have a long career. He was respected and well liked. He wrestled and made friends all over the world.

He spent about eight months in Amarillo, Texas in 1976. We spent a lot of time together in and out of the ring. Our friendship blossomed. I do miss his smile. He could always make me laugh.

Around 2000 Pez found out he had a bad heart. His life ended in a hospital waiting for a heart transplant. He was on the top of the list three different times and passed because he thought others deserved it more than he did. His heart finally gave out.

I wrote this story so that everyone would know that my dear friend Pez Whatley was a man!

He lived like a man and he died like a man. No one could more.

BAD WORDS

A man asked me if wrestling is phony,
he said it's like a show like dog and pony.
He got in my face and said it's all
baloney,
I said okay so why don't you try me?

Don't call me a phony or say I'm a fake,
those are two words I just can't take.
While I'm old now, I'm no piece of cake,
so leave me alone or your nose I might
break.

I'd eat you for breakfast now that is a
fact, you think you're a tough guy, I think
it's an act.
Go back where you came from, I'll help
you pack,
just say goodbye and don't ever come
back.

Dennis Stamp

3 FEAR

Fear is a natural emotion. It can be beneficial, it keeps us aware. Fear can generate adrenalin, which can magnify any situation. That might help you or make things a lot worse. You should be careful not to scare someone too much. And never back anyone into a corner.

The adrenalin caused by fear can give some people super human strength. It can freeze you solid mentally. Fear affects everyone differently. Fear can be a negative It can hold you back and hold you down. If you are male, fear is your worst enemy. No man of any age wants to be afraid of another man. I'm not saying that women like being afraid, they just deal with it differently.

I really wasn't afraid of the men I faced in the ring. I had a fear of failure. I didn't want to screw up a match. I'm not saying I could beat everyone. I just wasn't afraid.

By 1981, the M & M boys, Murdoch and Mulligan, had killed the Amarillo territory. It took them about two years. Amarillo had had weekly wrestling shows for over sixty years. The Funk brothers still lived in Amarillo; they were big stars all over the world.

I also lived in Amarillo, I still do. I had been a star in Colorado. Larry Lane wrestled in the Amarillo territory and was from Colorado.

Larry and the Funks got together and decided to run three wrestling shows in Colorado. Two towns on the east side of the Rockies and one on the west side.

I loved the idea. I hadn't had a match since Big Dick Murdoch told JJ Dillon to tell me I was fired. I loved being in the ring so much. To be in there with Dory, Terry and Larry was special to me beyond words. These guys were all great in the ring. They were a lot of fun to be with, especially Terry.

I wrestled Larry Lane the first night and everything went well.

We had to take the ring with us the next day to the town on the other side of the Rocky Mountains. The ring was pretty heavy. Broken down, the ring and its trailer weighed about 2500 pounds.

It was the middle of January and Colorado hadn't had much snow that year. In fact, the skies were crying about it. Wouldn't you know it, as soon as we leave, it starts to snow.

We had two vehicles. Terry ha a one ton pickup and Larry had a ¾ ton truck. Larry, being from Colorado, had tire chains. Terry, being from West Texas, didn't. Since Terry had the bigger truck, he pulled the ring. I jumped in Terry's front seat. What luck, I get to ride with Terry.

As we started up the mountains the snow starts really coming down. We were to cross the Rockies at Monarch Pass, elevation 11,000 feet.

The higher up we got the more it snowed. The visibility got worse and the road got slick. About halfway up the mountain the tires started to slide more. We were all over the road. It had become a blizzard.

No wrestling show is ever cancelled, for any reason. Turning back was not an option. There was no way to turn around. I was getting nervous. I could look out of the window and see about a thousand feet down. We spun a few times. We were still okay, but the weather kept getting worse. So, to keep from falling off the mountain, Terry starts to drive in the inside lane.

Here we are, driving up the Rocky Mountains, in a blizzard on the wrong side of the road. I hated going around curves blind. I was scared out of my mind. I begged Terry not to go around corners like that. Terry said if we stop we won't get started again.

I just shut up. Getting scared is bad enough, but staying scared is torture. I was so scared; I sweat right through my jacket.

We finally got up to Monarch Pass where we could pull off the road. I couldn't get out of Terry's truck fast enough! The man's crazy, I said, referring to Terry. He is the craziest person I've ever met. I can't ride with him anymore, I would rather walk.

So what did Terry say about it? "We made it didn't we."

"I'm riding with Larry" I said. "He's got tire chains and he's sane."

We switched the ring to Larry's truck because he had chains. And I got into Larry's truck for the ride down the mountain. There were four of us. Larry was driving; next to him was his wife. Next to Larry's wife was Vickie Funk, Terry's wife and I was by the door.

We hadn't gone far when Larry realized we were in a controlled skid. The road was snow packed. The ring trailer was so heavy it was pushing us down the mountain.

Once again, I could look out my window and see about a thousand feet down!

Larry Lane was one of the coolest men I've ever met. I knew he wouldn't panic. Larry's wife panicked. "Jump Dennis!" she shouted at me. "Jump or we'll all be killed!"

I tried to calm her down. "Larry's got it" I said. "He's as cool as ice. He's in control."

Larry didn't talk. He was locked into the road. Wow, I thought. Out of the frying pan and into another frying pan!

We had one close call. A semi had jackknifed about three feet into our lane. The car that was going around it stopped. Somehow we slid by.

(Fear) I was scared all the way up and all the way down the mountain.

We all made it.

That night when I took off my pant to put on my wrestling gear, I saw some bruises on my leg. There were four dime sized bruises on the inside of my thigh, and a slightly bigger bruise on the outside. I went over to where Terry was dressing. "Would you like to see your wife's finger prints?" I asked, showing him my leg.

I thought he would laugh. He didn't. He finally smiled and said "Don't worry, Stamp, after our match they won't show."

"Why not?" I asked.

"Because you'll have bruises all over your body" he laughed.

Even Terry Funk, the bravest man I've ever met and certainly one of the toughest couldn't scare me.

My trip over the Rocky Mountains had scared me so badly, that even a beating from Terry; the King of Hardcore Wrestling, would seem like a treat.

BILLY

William Arthur Robinson was the name he bore.
He was born on the first day of the 2nd world War.
He was always a fighter, right down to his core
No one could scare him, he'd only want more.

He traveled the world trying to find
A man who could wrestle, one of his kind.
He'd beaten the best, he made up his mind
On their reputations he wined and he dined.

This man became the Godfather I'd need.
He showed me the holds I'd never seen.
He beat me so; I thought he was mean,
He'd beat me more if ever I'd scream.

Real beatings he gave me, they weren't fake,
He was beating me up for my own sake.
To worry about a beating was the real mistake.
He taught how a beating to take.

The fear of a beating from me he freed.
It was something that I surely did need.
I love the man so much now you see,
He'll forever be (MY DADDY) to me.

Dennis Stamp

4 TOUGH GUY

It is surely every man's dream, especially young men, to be a tough guy. Whether they think so or not, survival is an instinct. I always wanted to be considered a tough guy. After wrestling in high school and college, I became a Professional Wrestler.

From the first time I saw wrestling in person I was hooked. I loved it. I still do. Professional wrestling is a different world. I've described it as a cross between "Alice in Wonderland" and "Peter Pans' Never-Never Land"

There are large men with good looks, great bodies and HUGE Egos. All these men think that they're THE alpha male. You mix that with large amounts of testosterone and it creates a macho world where like "Alice in Wonderland" Things are upside down and backwards. And like "Peter Pan's Never-Never Land", no one ever grows up. In fact inside the business the wrestlers are referred to as "The Boys".

The alpha male syndrome works on different levels in the business. Who is the toughest is debated endlessly in dressing rooms and the back seats of cars. There were almost never any fights. Most of the time talk is just talk. Some people start believing their own stories.

I had been wrestling in Amarillo about a week. It was a big Territory with Colorado Springs and Albuquerque, New Mexico to the west. Abilene, Childress and San Angelo, Texas were to the south. With Amarillo, Lubbock and Hereford right in the middle. The trips were long and the towns far apart, so the wrestlers rode together. It helped with the expenses and the boredom.

My first trip in the Territory was with Davy O'Hannon, Tom Stanton and Frank Goodish -AKA - Bruiser Brody. The trip got off to a bad start. Brody was thirty minutes late. I pointed out to him that there were three others who were all on time.

Bruiser Brody was a big guy, 6'4" and about 265 pounds. He had long shaggy hair, he looked like a caveman. He thought he was tough. He was convincing. A lot of people thought he was tough.

I was smaller than him. I was 6'2" and weighed about 225 pounds. I had a reputation. I had wrestled in college, trained with a Shooter (Billy Robinson) and had been the "office policeman" in three different territories.

We were on a long trip and Brody started in on me. "I'm not afraid of Shooters" he popped off. "Are you a Shooter, Stamp?"

Shooters were the elite of the amateur wrestlers. They could wrestle and they knew how to break bones. "No," I said calmly, not wanting any trouble. "I wrestled and played football in college" I replied.

We were on a five day trip and he kept digging at me more and more. He told stories of this one and that one that he'd beaten or scared. Some of them were college wrestlers.

"I'm afraid of no college wrestlers" he said smugly. "No college boys, period."

I didn't think I had the right to make a scene in someone else's car so I kept quiet. Now I imagine he thought I was afraid. I thought probably the other guys did too. We finally got back to Amarillo about three AM. We were in the parking lot of the Center City Motel downtown Amarillo. Brody got his bag out of the trunk of Davy's Cadillac. I got my bag out and I slammed it down.

I got right in the big Neanderthals face "Listen you big son of a bitch. You may well kick the shit out of me but we're gonna find out and we're gonna find out right now!

The bully coughed. He took about three steps backward and with a forced laugh, he said "I was just testing you, Stamp." He turned and walked away. He never bothered me again.

The whole scene reminded me of a Texas Hold'Em analogy. I had aces and I was 'all in'. Come to find out, Brody didn't have a pair.

Now this episode really boosted my reputation, especially in my own mind. I had been all over the country and halfway around the world. I was not afraid.

My reputation hurt me in the business. There is so much paranoia. I like it though, who wouldn't? I had a reputation for being a "Tough Guy" in the mucho, macho world of professional wrestling.

"Tough guy" certainly has its down side. First of all, it won't get you booked. People think that tough guys can't be very smart, but they can be mean and are dangerous. Like most stereotypes this is false. You'll be safer and generally treated nicer by a legitimate Tough Guy. Its bullies like Brody who pushed people around.

Having backed down Brody enhanced my reputation. He was bigger and stronger than me. He bragged about bench pressing over 400 pounds. I was lucky to bench press my own weight. But I could do about a thousand push-ups. I was in excellent shape.

Now I had a little more click in my step and held my nose just slightly higher. There were a few more little incidents. I once called out TWO Von Erick's. Neither Kevin, David nor both of them would face me.

About a year later the territory changed. Dick Murdock and blackjack Mulligan bought the territory. These were two big guys. Murdock at 280 pounds was a little bit at. Mulligan was 305 pounds and not fat. They thought they could run the territory. They were good in the ring, but they were no brain trust. They couldn't even run their own lives. They had no idea how to run a business. They had things screwed up form the start.

They didn't like me. They kept moving me down the card and cut my bookings. They wanted me to quit. I wouldn't. I had a wife and a daughter and I didn't want to go back on the road. Without much to lose, I went for broke. I asked to be the booker, a job I could do in my sleep. This became a big joke.

"Stamp's crazy. Who does he think he is anyway?" Word got around quickly. I heard about it in the dressing rooms. "Stamp" they said "is dumber than we thought." I finally had enough. I went to the office mad as hell. Blackjack was the only one there. I called the big man out like I had

Brody. Mulligan looked at me and started to laugh. He laughed so hard I thought he might break a window out of the office. I stood there a few minutes and started to walk away. By now I was laughing a little bit myself.

"Hey, Stamp" he hollered at me. "You got balls kid, I give you that."

Yeah, I thought and I'm glad I get to keep 'em. I walked away with my head slightly lower. Blackjack Mulligan was a legitimate "Tough Guy". Did he win? Of course, he won. Did I lose? Yes, maybe some of my attitude. To put it in poker terms I called him with my pair of aces. When I saw he had four Kings, I threw in my hand and went home.

One thing I know for sure. No matter how tough you think you are or how tough your really are. There is always some tougher.

POSTSCRIPT

Frank Goodish – AKA – Bruiser Brody was stabbed to death wrestling in Puerto Rico. He tried to bully the wrong guy.

Dick Murdock – AKA – Dirty Dick lived like there was no tomorrow until he made it come true. He died from a massive stroke at age 49.

Big Bob Windom – AKA – Blackjack Mulligan I hear he now weighs over 400 pounds. That's good to know. Now he'll never catch me.

THE GRIM REAPER

I went eyeball to eyeball.

With the Grim Reaper one night.

He had the blackest eyes.

Not a flicker of light.

I didn't blink.

Finally,

He said with a wink:

"I'll be back."

"It maybe sooner than you think."

Dennis Stamp

5 EGO

I was wrestling in Los Angeles in the mid Seventies. We had two live 90 minutes TV shows a week. I had a lot of matches and a lot of interviews. I was always a good talker. If anyone outside the business wanted to interview a wrestler, they got to talk to or more likely listen to me.

Louie Tillet was the booker. He was about 5'7" with built up soles and lifts inside his shoes. He was French Canadian so his accent fit well with his Napoleon complex. Louie had a job for me. Go talk at a Junior High School. That was ok with me, I knew I wouldn't get paid but I liked doing talks.

I went to see the office manager, Larry Korn. Larry had grown up in LA so he knew how to get everywhere. After he gave me directions he told me Louie wanted to see me.

"Stamp" Louie said, "Take S.D. Jones with you."

"Why?" I asked.

"You've seen his interviews, Stamp, Jones can't talk. You told me he could talk. He just stands there."

S.D. Jones was a real good guy. I liked him, everyone liked S.D. He had a great body and he was good in the ring. His problem was the camera. In the r=dressing rooms or on trips he was funny. He talked almost as much as I did. On camera he froze like a statue.

"He needs the practice" Louie told me. "Oh yeah, take the other African American with you." (He didn't use that term, he used another word.)

The other guy was the Mighty Zulu. He wrestled as an African warrior. He was not well liked by the other wrestlers. In fact he and I butted heads a few times. He had a bigger body than me but a real small head. Though I was smaller I have a big head. Needless to say brains always win. So I moaned to Larry "I have to take those TWO with me?

"It's not so bad, Stamp," Larry said. "Zulu has a car and he'll take Jones with him."

Good I thought, in this LA traffic that will save me about an hour.

The talk was in the auditorium of the Junior High School. They had three chairs set up for us on the stage. The other two finally got there - thirty minutes late. The school Secretary and the Principal were with us on the stage. I got the microphone and went first. I finished my talk and sat back down. They clapped, but not much. I looked around at the kids. Something wasn't right. I looked over to the school Secretary "Is this school for re...?" I paused.

"It's a school for special needs children" she interjected. Oh no, I thought. That's why I bombed. I didn't know my audience.

S.D. Jones went next. So what does he do? He took off his shirt and told the kids he "can bench press 420 pounds." This gets a big reaction. The kids liked that. That's all he said and he sat back down.

Next The Mighty Zulu got up to talk. He took off his shirt and told the kids he "can bench press 515 pounds". Once again it got a big reaction from the kids.

Now I'm mad. Not red hot mad, I'm white hot mad! These two dummies had upstaged me without even talking. My EGO kicked in. I jerked the microphone from Zulu. I started over. "Strength is very important in wrestling. Skill and knowledge of holds are also very important." As I said this I walked over to the Principal. He was a big man, maybe 200 pounds and he had on a suit and tie. He was probably the biggest man in these kids' lives.

With the microphone in one hand I Fireman's carried the Principal. Now I had him up on my shoulder and I was still talking calmly.

It got so quiet; I thought maybe people stopped breathing. When I gently

30

set him back down on his feet, the place went wild! The kids and teachers were all screaming.

It didn't matter to me that it was a Special Ed. Junior High, an audience is an audience; MY audience. No one steals the show from ME.

Now that's EGO.

HARLEY

His wrestling name was Handsome Harley Race.
He could back men down with the LOOK ON his
face.
He put good guys and bad guys INTO their place.
They called him "The King" he was really an ace.

He worked at the matches when he was fifteen.
No more school after what he'd seen.
He wanted to wrestle, he knew he was green.
He worked real hard at becoming mean.

I spent time with Harley in the ring.
The place where he truly was a king.
I fought hard but took a real beating.
That was during our very first meeting.

I turns out Harley is a real good guy.
Even though he fired me I knew why.
He was the new booker, he had to TRY
To get rid of trouble. I didn't cry.

Being the best was Harley's main game.
The fact that he got hurt was such a shame.
He gave us his body, no ones to blame.
He certainly made it into my Hall of Fame.

6 MOVIE STAR

The biggest movie star I ever met was Sylvester Stallone. It was after his first big hit, Rocky. His next movie was Paradise Alley. Rocky was a boxing movie and Paradise alley was about wrestling.

Terry Funk was trying to break into movies at that time. He met with Stallone and got a part in his movie. Terry was to be the main wrestling villain. To give the movie authenticity, Terry could provide wrestlers for the wrestling scenes.

Since Rocky was such a huge success, everybody wanted to be in Stallone's movie. For that matter most of us would be in any movie. Like most performers all wrestlers want to be stars. So this movie was going to be our big break.

Terry rounded up about twenty wrestlers. Eight of us came from Amarillo: me, Larry Lane, Tonya Kid, Ervin Smith, Alex Perez, the Lawman and a couple of other guys.

They flew us to Los Angeles in first class. We'd all flown before so we had walked through first class. But none of us had actually flown in first class. It was a fun trip. Can you imagine flying first class with your friends to Hollywood to be in a movie! Needless to say, everyone was pumped.

We got together when we got off the plane at LAX.

"Wow we're in Hollywood" one of the guys said. "When are we going to see some movie stars?"

I laughed. I had lived in L.A. I had been to that airport quite a few times. "It's Los Angeles" I said. "You don't see movie stars walking around. I've been to this airport before; I've never seen a star" I said in a teasing tone.

"C'mon guys, let's take the escalators down to get our bags."

As we were going down, I noticed someone on the up escalator. It was the tall man who played the part of the butler on the TV show "The Addams Family". His name on the show was Lurch.

For a moment he and I had direct eye contact. Not wanting to bother him, I mouthed the words "Hi, Lurch". He turned his head away so I pointed him out to the other wrestlers. They went crazy.

"Hey Lurch" and they continued with his tag-line "You rang?" This broke into a chorus mixed with laughter you could feel. When we got to the bottom of the escalator, they turned on me.

"You're so smart, Stamp. You said we wouldn't see any movie stars. We haven't left the airport and we saw him. We saw Lurch!" They stayed on me.

We checked into the Universal Sheraton Hotel, It was a part of the Universal complex. We each got our own big room. When I got to my room, the light on my phone was blinking.

Who knows I'm here? I wondered. It was a friend of mine who lived in L.A. Jerry Hernandez. Jerry had been the lead singer for the group "The Spiral Staircase". They had one big hit "I Love You More Today Than Yesterday". After the song became a hit, they fired Jerry. They were never heard from again.

"How did you know I was here?" I asked him.

"My mom still works for the L.A. airport. She saw Larry Kom from the L.A. Wrestling Office. He told her" was his reply.

Wow, I thought, some things never change. The rumor mill is alive and well. I had met Jerry at the wrestling matches. He liked wrestlers and we liked him.

"Come up and hang out with us." I said. "There are some great guys here you haven't met. If you can find us, we're way up on the tenth floor."

"Don't worry Stamp; everyone will be higher when I get there!"

"Yes," I thought "we could go up to the nineteenth floor. That would probably be as high as we could go"

When we left the tenth floor we went down to the dining room. Everybody ate. I guess all the excitement of being in Hollywood made everyone hungry. Some of the guys ate twice! We were wrestlers and wrestlers are always hungry.

There was a problem in the dining room after we left. Dick Murdoch took a bottle of wine from Telly Savalas' table. Can you imagine? Trying to steal from KOJAK! He wanted Murdoch kicked out of the hotel.

Once again, "Dickie" made us all look bad. We weren't allowed back in the dining room. We could only use the coffee shop.

Shortly after the Murdoch incident The Lawman (Don Slatton) and Dory Funk, Jr. go to the dining room and walked right in. The next morning I asked him "Don, how did you get in the dining room? I thought wrestlers were banned."

"The guy at the door did ask if we were wrestlers" he said.

"What did you say?" I asked.

"I didn't lie to him; I just showed him my badge".

"You carry your badge?" I asked.

"I am a Deputy Sherriff, you know, back in Abilene, Texas."

"Do you always carry your badge?" I asked.

Now he knew he had me. He was laughing hard.

"We didn't even have to pay." He continued, "We were comped."

I smiled and said "I thought Junior would buy your dinner."

"You haven't known the Funks as long as I have" he came back. By then he was doubled over with laughter.

We walked to the studio. It looked like a wrestler's arena, with a ring in the middle and rows of chairs around it. And that made us all feel more at home.

Two other actors from the movie went on to be stars. They were Armand Assante and Anne Archer. Each of the stars had a director's chair.

Stallone was the writer, producer, director, and star of the movie. His chair was two feet taller and made from hand tooled leather. The only person who ever sat in it was Anne. Sly (as it said on the back of the chair) was too busy to sit down.

I asked Terry if Anne was Stallone's wife. "No, she's just an actress" he replied.

Just an actress, I thought. No, she's drop dead gorgeous. When you look like that, you can sit anywhere you like.

The actor who played the part of Stallone's brother, the wrestler, was a real nice guy. He had been a boxer. He was 6'5", handsome and well built. He looked like a wrestler.

It seemed to me the first rule of the movie set was: Hurry up and wait. We got to the set at 8 am. And we then sat around for three hours. They had to shoot a couple of scenes. They were only about ten seconds long but they did each one about ten times. With so many people working it was like a beehive. There were three cameramen for each camera. There were actors, extras, soundmen, makeup artists and grips, whatever they are. They were all getting paid by the day or by the week. So they wanted to make the movie as long as they could.

The wrestlers got $300.00 a day. We all finished in one day. When they filmed the wrestling scenes, everyone watched. We each had ten to fifteen seconds. Of course, each wrestler wanted to show his best move. That went well for about the first eight of us.

I did my fireman's carry. His long legs up in the air, I landed him perfectly. He didn't feel a thing. All the actors who were watching the wrestling scene all "Oohed and Ahh'd". 'How did he do that?" I heard one of them ask.

This went well until Dory Funk, Jr. hit him with his under arm forearm. He bent him over and popped it off his chest. It made a "POP." I think it sort of scared the actor. It didn't hurt him. Stallone stepped up into the ring. He didn't like that. "We can add sound effects" he said with a big smile on his face.

So we changed direction. The year the movie took place was in 1946. Stallone's brother in the movie was an ice man during the day and a wrestler at night. He delivered ice with ice tongs. So his wrestling name was the "Ice Man". His finishing hold was called "The Ice Tongs". He would stand behind you and clamp his hands on your shoulders close to your neck. He would shake you back and forth then sling you.

Stallone wanted to demonstrate this move. I have always been the demonstrator guy, since Junior High. I got into the ring with Stallone; he wanted to show the wrestlers what to do. He put the hold on me. He shook me a couple of times and threw me. I took off like a rocket. I landed in a pile in the corner.

The first thing he did was look at me, and then he looked at his hands. He pointed at me "THAT'S IT!" he shouted. "That's what I want. That's exactly what I want!"

I made Sylvester Stallone "look". It was a small victory but a victory to me.

While I'm proud to have been in the movie, I didn't like it. When I saw the ringmaster with a red rubber nose, I knew it was wrong. I asked Terry about the rubber nose. "You don't understand, Stamp. These guys are real smart. They know what they're doing."

The movie bombed at the box office. If you should ever watch Paradise Alley my name is in the credits. To see me look closely, my back is to the camera.

BE FREE

If you get cancer you may try

to keep inside and wonder why

it's you and not some other guy

who sits around and waits to die.

Life is to me the place to be,

a paradise for you and me.

Just look skyward and you will see

a star, a bird, a big oak tree.

I don't have the time to cry

and I have yet to say goodbye,

so on myself I must rely.

And once again I'll learn to fly.

So please for me,

Don't
Ever
Cry

7 HAYSTACK CALHOUN

TWO OUT
OF
THREE

First of all, he was the biggest person I ever met in my life. He was about 6'3" and he weighed 640 pounds. He had to weigh himself at butcher shops, the ones that had the big scales.

He was as nice as he was big. He was always fun to be around. He could talk. He was a great interview. His character was this huge country boy. He wore bib overalls and called everyone "Neighbor".

He was from Tucumcari, New Mexico. When he was seventeen he weighed 450 pounds. Two different doctors told him he wouldn't live past the age of twenty. "What do those doctors say now?" I asked. "Oh, they both died over twenty years ago" he replied, trying not to laugh. "But you're still here" I blurted out. That broke him up with laughter. When Stacks laughed, everyone laughed. That's how it was traveling with Haystack, he was so much fun. We laughed all the time.

He drove a large Suburban. He had the front seat moved back so he could fit behind the wheel. You didn't want to ride in the backseat, there was no leg room.

"You know why I bought this big van don't you? he asked.

"Sure," I said. "You need something big."

"No, not that Neighbor. Lift up that lid in the back" he said.

"Wow" I said. He had a complete bar in the back.

"Yeah, Neighbor, I've got vodka, gin bourbon and Southern Comfort. What's your pleasure?" he asked.

"Thanks, Stacks, but I don't drink" I said.

"YOU DON"T DRINK?" he hollered. "What's wrong with you?"

"Oh, I know" he sat back and smiled. "You young guys all smoke that wacky tobacky. Don't you Neighbor; I'll get some of that."

That was in Georgia.

We met again a few years later in Amarillo. Promoters would bring in Haystack for a week or two and book Battle Royals all over the territory. A Battle Royal is a match with all the wrestlers in the ring at the same time. Usually there would be 10 to 14 wrestlers, but there could be as many as 20.

The match was an "Up the Pole" Battle Royal the night we wrestled in Lubbock, Texas. There was a pole, about fifteen feet high, attached to one of the ring posts. At the top of the pole was a money bag. The object of the match was to climb the pole and get the money.

I'd never heard of one before. Anyway, here I am 'the make it happen' guy. No one was going near the pole, with one exception – Haystack was camped out in that corner.

I got to the pole and climbed about halfway to the top. I was about 10 to 12 feet off the cement floor when one of Haystacks big paws grabbed the back of my tights and pulled down. I was holding onto the pole with my right hand and the front of mu trunks with my left as I mooned the entire city of Lubbock!

So, finally, I dropped to the floor and rolled under the ring to pull up my trunks.

Boy was I mad!

Stacks roared with laughter. I was so mad; I swore I'd get even. Well here goes:

I'm telling a Haystack story. I'd heard it a few times from different people and I thought it was really funny. I finally met Chief Bigheart. He was actually with Haystack when this happened. He told me the whole story.

Haystack was a big star on the east coast in the late 50s, early 60s. Haystack and the Chief were flying from New York to Washington, DC. Before they got on the plane, one of the other wrestlers shoo-flyed Haystacks drink. (Shoo-fly is a strong laxative for cattle)

On the plane they had to take out an armrest so Stacks could have two seats. The plane no more than gets off the ground and Stacks has to go. The bathrooms on airplanes are small for normal sized people. Haystack could not fit through the door. The Chief said he was mashing on that big belly when those marbles hit the floor.

What a smell! It was painful. One stewardess came to the back of the plane and when she saw what had happened and got a whiff – she threw up. Another stewardess fainted.

They finally found a mailbag and the Chief held it for him while a stewardess held up a sheet to cover the back of the plane. Tears were streaming down her face.

"It smelled so bad" the Chief said, "the oxygen masks dropped down."

"Maybe the captain dropped them" O said.

"No, he was in the front with the door closed. The smell brought down the masks" the Chief insisted. "I was there" he said "I'll never forget that smell."

I'll never forget that story.

The last time I saw my friend was in Odessa, Texas. Haystack was no longer a big attraction, now he was just big. He was getting older and had some health issues. He knew his days in the ring were numbered.

The match was me against Haystack in Odessa.

"You're going over Neighbor" he said. "What do you want to do?"

"I can't pin you Stacks, it's too unbelievable. What about a count out?" I asked. "I bail out of the ring to keep from getting pounded and you come out after me. I slide back in the ring quickly and you get counted out."

"That's it?" he asked.

"Well, the office wanted me to hit you in the head with a chair" I said.

"That makes more sense to me" Haystack said. "You'll get more heat and I'll have a reason to get counted out."

"Okay," I said. "If that's all right with you."

"Fine" he said. "I've been looking forward to this match."

"To what?" I popped off.

"To show you I can wrestle with you college boys."

"College boys?" I asked in a tone.

"Guys like you and Jack Briscoe. You think you're so good. You couldn't even get behind me."

"Oh yes I could Stacks" I said. "It would just take me a day and a half to get there."

"Laugh now" he said. "We'll see. We'll see who laughs later."

The match went well. I had a lot of heat in Odessa. The fans were into the match. With about 8 or 9 minutes gone we were faced off in the middle of the ring.

"I thought you could get behind me" Stacks teased.

Before he got the words out of his mouth, I was behind him. I couldn't lock my hands; I couldn't even get my arms around him. While I was trying to hold onto him he drove me straight back into the corner turn buckle.

I didn't see it coming. It hurt like hell. I dropped to the canvas, then to the floor. He came out after me. I found a metal folding chair and hit him in the head. I got back in the ring and Stacks got counted out.

Now my ribs really hurt. I could feel pain with every breath.

I went to Haystacks' dressing room more than a little bit mad. "You broke my ribs" I said. It even hurt to talk.

"Your ribs aren't broken, Neighbor. They may be bruised but you'll get over it."

With that big grin on his face I was finding it hard to be mad. But my ribs were killing me.

Stacks started laughing. He looked over at me and laughed some more. "There's one thing you little guys never learn" he said.

"And what's that?" I asked sarcastically.

"You believe me now? Size does matter." He again roared with laughter.

I had to leave the room. It hurt too much to laugh. As I limped back to my dressing room it all came back to me.

The fat man had gotten me again.

WRITING ON THE WALL

I can read the writing on the wall.
It's not over; it's late in the fall.
I'm still here, still standing tall,
I'll do what it takes just give me a call.

The people in power say "You have no name"
And "You know the rules and won't play the game"
"To be like the others you must look the same"
"Just look in the mirror, that's who is to blame."

Go sit in a corner is what you can do,
Or just hold your breath until you turn blue.
Don't sit and simmer in your own stew,
Stand up like a man, start something new.

It won't work to move or stay in your place,
Those wrinkles you earned look good on your face.
You look good through you no longer race,
The twenty year olds have too fast a pace.

When you were younger you were quite bold,
Now you no longer come in from the cold.
There's no fool like an old fool I am told,
You must face the facts, you're just too old.

8 BRYANT GUMBEL

His name is pronounced like its spelled. Gum Bel. I know as a kid his friends must have called him Gum Ball. I wasn't there, but I was a kid once and with a name like Stamp I was a target myself.

I was wrestling in Los Angeles. The year was 1975. The times were changing. The TV networks wanted to keep up with the times and there were no African American newscaster. NBC was grooming Bryant for the network. He was on KNBC, the network station in Los Angeles.

Along with newscasts, Bryant had his own segment called "Be What You Want To Be." The premise was people would write or call into the station with their dream job and KNBC would set it up and have Bryant host it. Someone wanted to be a mayor so they found a small town where he was made mayor for the day. One man wanted to be a fireman. He got to put on all the fireman's gear and ride on the back of a fire truck.

This was a classy show. When someone wanted to be a baseball player they went to the LA Dodgers and he was able to take batting practice. So, naturally, when someone wanted to be a professional wrestler, KNBC called Mike LaBell, the LA wrestling promoter. They wanted to know if they could bring their show to the Olympic Auditorium and film their man in the ring with a professional wrestler. We had a meeting about this so called "match" where Louie Tillet, who was the booker, told us what the TV station wanted.

"Wrestle who?" one of the guys asked.

"I don't know his name, all I know is he's 6'2" and weighs about 250 pounds. Oh yeah" he continued, "It's a free shot. You won't get paid."

This was the lifeline the other wrestlers were looking for. "No money, no way" was the common response. I don't have to name names; there was only one person who would do it. That was me. I wasn't afraid of getting hurt. I had a reputation and was putting it on the line. I always worried about looking bad, so mostly this was just another performance for me.

Bryant got there with his TV crew. I'd never seen him before. He was handsome, articulate and very smooth. I liked him immediately. He asked me if he could interview me.

"Sure" I said.

"I'd like to film about 3 minutes and edit it down to 2 minutes" he said.

"I know, cut out the dead spots" I said.

"Ah, ah" he said back. "I'm not saying there are going to be dead spots," not wanting to insult me. I wasn't insulted. I saw the interview later; they didn't cut a single word.

This exhibition match was held at the Olympic Auditorium, downtown Los Angeles. Before the match Bryant asked me not to hurt the man. The owner, Mike LaBell, echoed that. Unfortunately for me, the booker didn't feel the same way. On my way to the ring, Louie stopped me.

"I want a broken bone" he said. "I don't care; you can break an arm or a leg." Then he walked away.

The seats in the arena were all empty, except for one. The man's wife, holding their six month baby ringside, was sitting in the front row. I didn't meet the man. The first time I saw him was in the ring. He didn't impress me. He was probably 250 pounds, but he looked kind of fat to me.

The first thing I did was one of my signature moves. I fireman carried him. In that instant I knew he was mine. I pinned him three times. He tapped out, or actually screamed out another three times. I dominated him completely. He got nothing.

The whole thing took about three minutes. Bryant was smiling, he liked it very much. LaBell was happy that Gumbel was happy. The booker, Louie Tillet, walked out. He wouldn't talk to me he was so mad. I was supposed to be his pistol. What good was it if you couldn't pull the trigger?

In my mind I had done it the best possible way. I totally dominated. Besides, he hadn't smarted off or laughed or smirked. I had no reason to injure him; especially with his wife and baby sitting right there. When I went to the dressing room, the wrestlers came out of hiding. There must have been ten or twelve of them watching the show. They were all mad. A couple of them read me out.

"You should have hurt him!" was pretty much all I heard. These are the same people who wouldn't do the "match". They didn't even show their faces at the taping.

So, what I got in the dressing room was the silent treatment. No wrestlers would talk to me. This only lasted a couple of days.

KNBC liked the segment so much they showed it at least three separate times. About two weeks after the Bryant Gumbel episode, Louie called me into his office.

"Garibaldi is my new assistant booker. Stamp, I've got you booked in Vancouver."

Did that hurt? Yes, it did. I had come to LA with Louie. I had stayed at his house; he'd stayed at mine. I thought we were friends. I talked wrestling matches endlessly with him. I'd have two matches on almost every card AND tons of interviews. I worked really hard to build up the territory and I had.

"I had you running the towns" Louie shouted at me.

I didn't know what was going on in them. "What do you mean, Louie?" I asked.

"I want to know every word said in the dressing room." He snapped.

"I'm not a stooge, Louie," I replied.

"You're not a stooge when you work for the office. That's part of your job."

I loved it in LA; the fans, the weather, the beaches. I could have done that job forever. Garibaldi was in and I was out. Leo had talked his way into the territory as a referee. He was like the man in the O'Jays song "The Backstabbers". He smiled in your face. He smiled all the time. He had been an old co-worker of Louie's they shared the same idea: survive at any cost. Leo started when he got there. He would tell Louie what the guys were talking about in the dressing room. It got so bad we would see him standing behind a door, listening to us.

One night a movie producer sent a writer to talk to a wrestler. He wanted to make a movie about wrestling. The catch was the only wrestler the producer wanted to talk to was me. It was fine with me. I liked to do interviews. We sat in the empty arena when I started talking, I pointed out a man (Garibaldi) standing near us in a doorway.

"What's he doing?" the writer asked me.

"He was sent here to listen to me." I replied.

"What for?" he asked.

"In case I say anything about anything."

"Why are they so paranoid?" he asked.

"You'll have to ask them." I said.

"I don't think so" he said as he gathered his things "I wont' work like this."

He turned to me looked me right in the eye and said: "I want to talk to you, alone. I'll call you" as he walked away. He never called.

Besides being a willing and able stooge, Leo had a plan. He was close with the Guerreo family. There were four brothers who wrestled. He would bring them to LA and go after the Latino fans. I didn't have a problem bringing in Chavo. You can't have too many stars.

Louie wanted me out. Leo Garibaldi for sure wanted me out. I went to see the owner, Mike LaBell. He wasn't real bright. He depended on the bookers. They told him I was too big, that the fans would be confused, and they wouldn't know who to cheer for. They were right about one thing, at 6'2" and 230 pounds I did make the Guerros look small.

It didn't matter. Nothing mattered now. I was gone. To where: to Vancouver, British Columbia; the purgatory of professional wrestling.

After a few months, Louie was gone. He ended up driving a taxi in Miami. It took Leo a couple of years to kill the Los Angeles territory.

Now it's gone, long gone.

I'm still here telling my side of the story.

I accept full responsibility for all of my actions.

I should have known how the game was played.

I learned a good lesson AND I got to work with Bryant Gumbel.

FEELINGS

It's undeniable to me that I love an audience
And audiences love me.
Emotion is what I always bring,
You see what I feel, I feel everything.

The ring is such a perfect stage,
With an audience to engage.
It doesn't matter what your age,
You'll never want to turn the page.

The chairs which seat people around ringside
They're power circles, that can't be denied.
So you can draw power by being inside,
And use that power so it's on your side.

I felt so much power inside the ring.
I love it more than anything.
The power was love through fans eyes.
A love that's one of life's greatest highs.

9 THE MATCH

Saturday October 30th, 1976

The date alone was ominous to me. It was Halloween eve, a full moon and the sixth anniversary of my mothers' passing. Then, there was the building, The Bull Barn in Hereford, Texas. True to its name, had many cattle feed lots. The Bull barn was in the middle of them.

Hereford was the smallest town in the Amarillo territory. It ran every other Saturday. It was set up as a place for the wrestlers to work who came in for TV. It's about forty five miles from Amarillo. It was a place to work close to home on a Saturday night. Dory Funk, SRs' ranch was near Umbarger, about halfway between Hereford and Amarillo.

The Match, Dennis Stamp vs. Dory Funk, JR was set up for a reason. The referee was the reason. Stanley Marsh 3, a wealthy, eccentric, world traveler and big game hunter. He was a patron of the arts, and an artist himself.

Marsh's best known work of art is the Cadillac Ranch, just outside of Amarillo on Interstate 40. It is ten Cadillac's planted in the ground. The cars are each a different year from the fifties, when America made the best. And Cadillac was king.

Sports illustrated wanted to interview Mr. Marsh. The problem was the magazine requires all subjects to be about sports. Stanley Marsh was to referee the wrestling match to qualify for a magazine article. The wrestling promoter thought that by doing this favor he'd get our TV show on Marsh's station. (No TV deal ever happened.)

The match was not promoted. There were no TV interviews, no TV ads, and no ads of any kind. There were no TV cameras at the match, no cameras at all.

THE WRESTLER: Dory funk, JR

He had been an all-American football player in college. He was the N.W.A. World Heavyweight Champion for four and a half years. He defended his world title over a thousand times. The most Championship matches of any kind, anywhere, ever.

I idolized Dory.

Son of the popular Dory Funk, SR, he practically grew up in the ring. Learning everything he could from a true maestro, his father. Dory, JR became a master professional wrestler himself. He always carried his fathers name with a lot of class.

THE WRESTLER: Dennis Stamp

An all American football player and college wrestling champion. I was trained as a pro by Verne Gagne and Billy Robinson. Billy was considered the toughest man in the world. He was. He literally beat me up every day. After a few weeks I realized that the fear of a beating was worse than the beating itself. So he beat most of the fear out of me. I soon found out that everyone is afraid. By not being afraid I got a reputation for being a tough guy. And since I didn't believe the "songs" the bosses would sing to me, I got tagged with a bad attitude. Everything that I said was magnified and misquoted – And I've always had a lot to say.

At that time I'd had between 1200 and 1500 matches. I was totally at home in the ring. My ring character was an arrogant heel, a vicious, violent villain. I was a slow walkin', slick talkin', cocky bad guy.

I was trying to make a name for myself in West Texas. It was the backyard of the Funk Brothers, both World Champions.

When I was asked to do the match I didn't hesitate. "Absolutely" I said.

DRESSING ROOM

The whole night was surreal. I was alone in the heel dressing room most of the night. With the exception of the old referee, Ken Farber, who kept coming in and out. He always teased me, but that night he hit the jackpot.

"Remember, Stamp" he would say "Marsh is worth 60 million dollars so don't you touch 60 million dollars and you don't hurt 60 million dollars."

He finally made me mad. "I have never hurt a Referee," I yelled. I calmed right down. "I could make an exception in your case Farber."

Farber started for the door. "Wait" I yelled.

"What?" he asked abruptly.

"What are we doing? What's the finish? How long are we supposed to go?" I asked.

"Junior wouldn't say. He said you'd know what to do."

Wait Farber, Ask him" I said.

"He won't talk and you won't shut up. You're supposed to be a smart guy Concordia College. You figure it out."

THE MATCH

Dory and I got into the ring with little fanfare.

Here comes Stanley Marsh. He had on a tuxedo with tails, a top hat and tennis shoes. He looked like the Mad Hatter. How appropriate, I thought. He is prepared to go through the looking glass.

Pro wrestling was truly a wonderland. It was filled with strange and weird characters and sacred cows everywhere. Some of them made a few dollars, but nobody made much sense.

I wasn't surprised by his outfit and no one seemed to laugh. The crowd was light, maybe 150 people. There were empty seats at ring side. Normally I would have been upset. But that night I barely noticed and didn't care. I had a 60 million dollar audience.

The match was a contrast of styles.

Dory, the local hero, was the perfect protagonist. He was a nice guy, polite and humble, wore a cowboy hat and listened to Country/Western music.

I was a natural antagonist. I was brash, cocky and arrogant, a hard rock fan wearing a hippie headband.

I had wrestled in high school and college. I knew a lot of holds and moves. I started the match with a fireman's carry and kept a hold of his arm.

He stood up and reversed the arm bar into a hammerlock.

"Whoa" I thought, this guy can really wrestle. He's not letting me have anything. He's not blocking me. I would take the hold I wanted, and then he'd take it back. It was back and forth. I probably emptied my book of moves. We were both getting tired. The audience was dead quiet. Marsh was just standing there watching.

Being the action man and being the villain, I had to get Marsh involved in the match. So I pushed Dory into the ropes and held him there. This would call for the referee.

Marsh stepped up slowly and sort of stuttered "Ah – ah br – br – break the hold."

Without moving anything but my head, I turned to the side and in a loud deep voice I said "WHAT DID YOU SAY?"

I thought I saw two black tails. When I looked again, he was gone. He had bailed out of the ring. I looked at Dory, who had a tiny smile on his otherwise stone face.

Me, I totally lost it. "Hit me" I hissed at Dory under mu breath. He punched me in the head. I went straight down on my face. I began to laugh. I held my arms over my head to cover my face and hold myself down. I was laughing so hard, the ring was bouncing. It was the only time in my adult life that I can remember being overcome by a fit of laughter.

No one in the audience knew and Marsh for sure didn't know.

When I got back up, I looked at Dory and I lost it again. "Kick me" I said. He kicked me in the stomach and I went down again. I held myself down. I laughed out all the nerves and all the pressure.

This tine when I got up off the mat it was like I had gone through the looking glass. I was watching the match while it was happening. I was seeing it in slow motion.

The first thing I did was kick Junior hard in the stomach. Now it was on. As he bent over, I clenched my hands together and hit him with both arms. I grabbed a hold of his arm and forced him to the mat. I liked to work in and out of holds.

I knew that Amarillo was a punch and kick territory. Dory could punch and kick with the best of them. I would punch and kick with anyone.

So, I rolled his arm out to a bar and I dropped an elbow on his shoulder. As he got up off the mat, I kicked bootlace marks on his shoulder.

That made him mad.

He jerked his arm away from me. He came back at me with a forearm across my chest. It knocked me back. I rushed forward and he scooped my leg. He dropped elbows on my leg. He kicked me twice in the thigh. The bootlace marks looked like miniature railroad tracks. He then clamped a hold on my leg. When he finally stood up to drop all of his weight on me, I swung my free leg and caught him in the ribs, knocking him back. I got up quickly as he came toward me.

I scooped him up and body slammed him to the mat. This was to set him up for my big shot.

THE CHOP

The chop is an open hand which lands on an opponent's chest. It was a good move for me. I have long arms and I would twist my body half way around. Everyone could see it. If I cup my hand just slightly, and land it flat, it makes a pop. A little bit of sweat and a big swing con make a real big POP!

Anyway, I threw it hard, maybe too hard. I hurt my hand, it had to hurt Dory. He didn't go down. I lined him up again. This time it's perfect and popped big time. He still didn't go down. I'm a little hot now. My best shot landed perfectly, but he wouldn't go off his feet. I grabbed his arm and threw him into the ropes. As he came off the ropes, I hit him with a big chop that included my whole arm. He went down that time. I jumped to cover him for a pin. One, two, and he kicked out.

We faced off again. He came up with an arm bar. He slid his hands down to my wrist and again planted that big boot on my thigh. It really hurt. I kind of limped to shake it off.

He came at me with something I hadn't seen in the ring before. He hit me in the side of the head with a flipper. It's one way football players used to block. I didn't see it coming. It felt like an electric shock all through my body.

I felt like a cat in a cartoon getting my tail stuck in a light socket. I was frozen in place. I couldn't move. I could see and hear. I was wide awake, but I could not move.

I thought Junior took this as a slight; it was his finishing hold when he first started wrestling once he'd come out of football, everyone flew when he used that move.

I couldn't feel a thing or move at all.

So he hit me with it again and I was glad he did. All of my feeling came back but I still didn't go down, I couldn't. The third time he bounced off the ropes and ran into me with it I did a 180 degree flip almost landing on my head.

When I got up he grabbed me in a headlock. He bent to my ear and called a double knock out. I thought it strange at the time. I deferred to the master. I pushed him off into the ropes. When he came off the ropes we just barely hit heads.

BANG! Down I went with a thud. I looked over at Junior to see where we were going with this.

Dory didn't go down. Then I saw it, a small red spot. He looked like he was trying to hide it. But it was too late, I saw it. It was blood. One thing I knew about blood is it makes any situation more dramatic. It doesn't matter, car crash, bar fight or you accidently cut yourself, and the sight of blood heightens human emotion.

Sure enough, Dory was bleeding. I knew where I was going now.

By now Dory's body was covered with boot marks. His chest striped red and welting from all the Chops. Now I had only one target, his blood.

I threw a big round right at his head. The holds were over now.

The match became a fistfight. I hit him two or three times in the head. With each punch he staggered. He finally went down. I covered him for a pin. One, two, and he kicked out. I knocked him down again and again. Two count only, it takes three for a pin.

I slammed him near the corner. I got up on the second rope to drop a knee on his head. He moved. I landed on my knee. Now I am rolling around on the mat holding my leg.

He's up now and coming after me. I scrambled to get up, but he kicked my leg out from under me. He then proceeded to stomp my leg. Drop a knee in my thigh and kick my let a couple more times.
Page 8

Then he went for it.

THE SPINNING TOE HOLD

His father, Dory SR used it. His brother Terry, World champion at the time, used it. It's a submission hold. A Funk would take hold of your leg while you were on your back. They would then spin on it until you gave up.

So, Dory spun once. As he got half way around the second time I pushed him off with my other foot. He hit the ropes and dove straight at me. I put up my feet to flip him over, which I did. He held onto my ankles and I was bent in half with both shoulders flat on the mat.

Now I knew, Dory certainly knew and Stanley Marsh knew. One, two, three – the match was over.

I kicked out hard and slid out of the ring. I looked back to see Dory's hand being raised above his bruised and bloody body.

My hands hurt from hitting him. Other than that, I felt no pain. I had been in a tough match. It was the match of my life. To quote my friend tiger Nelson "It was a masterpiece, truly a masterpiece."

AFTERWARD

Stanley Marsh 3, the bravest man in the ring that night, got his interview with Sports Illustrated. He opened with something like this: "I've been all over the world. Never in my life have I seen two bigger, stronger, tougher men than Dennis Stamp and Dory funk, Junior."

I laughed at the time. But now I know he was right.

POLITICIANS

The Congress, the Senate, the Govs and the rest,
To live in the spotlight it's all they ask.
There's fame and glory in which they will bask,
Staying in office is their only task.

To change things people tell me to vote,
But who to vote for, some other dope?
Your choices are fear and hatred, not hope,
These monkeys just dance and swing on a rope.

The rope the Pols want is coated with gold,
To get your vote now, your hand they will hold.
Don't look in their faces, their eyes are ice cold.
Their hearts and their souls, they've already sold.

The media would like us all in one tent,
To tell us the stories and lies they invent.
Then tell us the next day that's not what they
meant,
The truth is they all work for the "One Percent".

10 TERRY AND BRECK

TAG-TEAM PARTNERS

FOREVER

I came to Amarillo over thirty years ago as a Professional Wrestler. When I was no longer booked, I started my own business. I owned and ran a pest control company.

One day while spraying a house, I noticed a young boy, about 8 years old, lying on the couch. I knew it was a school day. For conversation I asked his mother "Is he sick?"

"Yes" his mother told me. "Breck has malignant brain tumors and th doctors have given him thirty days."

Wow, I thought to myself. I've always got to open by big mouth.

As I walked through the boys' bedroom I saw a wrestling poster on the wall. Okay, I thought I can talk about wrestling. After I finished spraying, I went back to the mother. "I see your son is a wrestling fan" wanting to change the subject!

"Yes," she answered. "He loves wrestling. Terry Funk is his favorite. In fact, meeting Terry is on the top of his Make-A-Wish list." "Do you know

Terry?" she asked.

"Sure" I came back. "I wrestled Terry five times when he was World Champion." I never missed a chance to brag about that.

"Well" she tells me as I'm leaving "I have a friend who has Terry's phone number."

"Okay" I replied. "If you can't get a hold of him, give me a call." I hadn't talked to Terry for a few months, but we've always had each other's phone number. I wouldn't give it out, but I would call him.

Sure enough, Brecks mother called the next day. The doctors had downgraded her son from thirty days to day to day. And she couldn't get Terry's phone number.

I called Terry and he answered the phone. I explained the situation and how much this boy, Breck, wanted to meet him.

"Yes, I will" terry said.

"Can you go tomorrow?" I asked.

"Yes" he said. "If you go with me since I don't know those people."

I called the mother to let her know.

"Breck is so weak he can hardly hold his head up off the pillow" was all she said.

"We'll be there tomorrow" I assured her.

Terry and I met and went to Brecks' house. I went up to the door first. I knocked and the mother came to the door.

"It's terry" she said loudly. Now I could see Breck. "TERRY FUNK" he screamed and he jumped off the couch.

Our visit lasted about an hour. We talked and laughed. At one point we moved the coffee table and got down on the floor to demonstrate a few holds. Breck balled up a fist to show us how he would do it.

Terry showed more character. He asked Breck if he would be his tag-team partner.

"What does that mean?" Breck asked.

"It means I'll have your back" Terry told him.

Breck paused, and got a strange smile on his face. "Does that mean I"ll have your back too?" he asked.

"It sure does" Terry replied.

Now, Terry didn't go there empty handed. He had a poster of himself and a t-shirt. He signed them to Breck. As we were leaving the house, Terry said to Breck "Remember now, we're tag-team partners."

"I know" said Breck. "And I've got your back."

As we drove away from the house we were both quiet.

"I can't believe how tough that boy is" Terry finally said.

"Yeah" was all I could say. We didn't talk about the visit anymore.

About a year later, I ran into Brecks mother. We almost did a double knock-out. We recognized each other immediately and hugged.

"Dennis" she said. "I want to thank you so much for all you did for my son."

"It was Terry" I said.

"Yes" she said, "but you brought him to us."

"Well, how did things turn out?" I asked.

"Breck lived for two weeks after your visit. He wore the t-shirt every day. He only took it off to wash it, and then he would lay on the dryer until it was dry. He had to go Hospice for his last two days" she told me. "The only way Breck would agree to go was if he could take the poster with him."

"We buried him with Terry's poster" she said starting to tear up. "God bless you and Terry" she said and she walked away.

Some years later I was diagnosed with cancer. I had gone to the hospital with heart failure. My heart actually stopped twice in the emergency room.

The doctors discovered cancer. I had 4th stage fast growing lymphoma. There is no 5th stage.

I even heard the word Hospice used in one of their discussions. It was like being blocked in a corner. If my heart didn't get me then the cancer would.

The next day was hectic. Nurses, doctors, aides, specialists in and out of my room. And a long list of family and friends, many coming by to say goodbye. I didn't have time to think, let alone worry.

By 11 o'clock that night they were all gone. Now I was alone. There was a soft knock on my door. Who could that be? I wondered.

He stepped inside the door. It was Terry. It was Terry Funk.

I was blown away.

With him he brought 40 years of friendship. As Professional Wrestlers that's at least two lifetimes.

That visit was the best medicine I could have gotten. We laughed for three solid hours. Terry hadn't come to say goodbye, he come to let me know he had my back. And to remind of who I was. A Wrestler.

As Terry was leaving I saw him. I saw Breck. He was sitting on Terry's shoulder. He was smiling, he seemed so happy.

Then it hit me. I got chills, goose bumps all over my body.

It was Breck.

I had taken Terry to Breck when he needed him the most. So Breck brought Terry to me when I needed him so badly.

I finish this story where I started:

Terry and Breck, Tag-Team Partners, FOREVER.

I know, I'm living proof.

BOOKED

I flew here from across the sea,
A special trip it is for me.
Scotland is the place to be,
A country where all men are free.

My Scottish fans I love you so,
Your prayers and love helped me to go.
Chris Duke is my friend that you know,
He's gotten me booked with David Low.

I didn't die and go to Heaven.
I'm still alive, my motor's revvin'.
I've been a wrestler since eleven,
Booked again at sixty-seven.

Glasgow, Scotland
The Toughest City
In
The
World.

THANKS

Cover Designed by Bradley Craig, Contact: bradleycraig@hotmail.co.uk
All Photo's from Dennis Stamp personal collection and David J Wilson.
Chris Duke for being a wonderful friend, and standing with me through thick and thin.

19630918R00046

Made in the USA
San Bernardino, CA
06 March 2015